To Carol,

[illegible] ory Verse

[illegible] e-side.

[illegible] undaySchool

1973.

DEPUTY MUM

DEPUTY MUM

by

DENNIS W. BOREHAM

VICTORY PRESS
LONDON and EASTBOURNE

ISBN 0 85476 107 1

Printed in Great Britain for
VICTORY PRESS (Evangelical Publishers Ltd.),
Lottbridge Drove, Eastbourne, Sussex,
by Richard Clay (The Chaucer Press), Ltd.,
Bungay, Suffolk

CONTENTS

CHAPTER ONE

A BAD BEGINNING

"So I wish you all a very happy holiday."

The headmistress concluded her speech and stepped down from the stage. Five hundred girls tried to keep silent until she left the hall, but they were too excited. A gentle murmur of subdued voices began from the front and swept quickly through the assembled ranks to the rear, ebbing and flowing like the waves of the sea, until the murmur became a hubbub.

The teachers smiled. They understood. Wasn't it the last day of term? The new term was six whole weeks away; a thousand hours. Studies should be, and could be, laid aside.

Alison made her way towards the rear of the hall. She was in the middle school and didn't have to wait so long as the younger girls who were badly placed for a quick exit. She struggled along the aisle and up the steps into the foyer. Other girls pushed alongside her until the mass split up into smaller groups en route for their form rooms. Then she was with her special friends.

"When do you go?" one of them asked. "Pretty soon, isn't it?"

Alison nodded and smiled.

"On Saturday," she replied.

"Lucky you!"

Alison smiled again.

"It will be great!" she admitted. "I wish all of you could come with me. Wouldn't it be marvellous if you could?"

The other girls agreed.

"It's the south coast for me," one said, rather wistfully. "I shall be playing with my brothers on the beach and having to queue for ice creams."

Alison didn't know what to say. She knew what her friend meant. It wasn't a very exciting sort of holiday, especially if the English climate lived up to its reputation.

"It won't rain where you are going to," another girl said, seeming to read Alison's thoughts. "Don't forget to take your sun lotion. You are sure to need it."

"I hope I have thought of everything," Alison said. "It's difficult to know exactly what to take. I'm only allowed a suitcase and one medium-sized bag. Mother said we would have to pack all the things carefully, and I think we made the most of the space."

They reached their room and dawdled over collecting their things, for they were not in any hurry to part. Alison walked over to the huge windows and looked out across the park which bordered the school grounds. The leaves on the trees were like outstretched hands swaying, this way and that, in the summer breeze. When the girls returned to school the leaves would be less green, drier and curling at the edges, nearly ready to take their autumn plunge to the soft earth below.

"Strange, isn't it?" one of the girls said. "We spend all term wishing we were on holiday and then, when we can go home early and enjoy ourselves, we hang around the classrooms until one of the staff sends us on our way."

Alison turned away from the window.

"Let's go," she suggested. "It is rather silly to stay here, I suppose."

They picked up their bags and blazers and walked out into the hot sun. The traffic roared up the hill, stirring up the dust, making the air heavy with fumes.

"The south coast will be wonderful after this," one girl joked. "Cheer up, Carol. You would hate to spend all your holiday here."

They all laughed.

"London is getting noisier and noisier," someone said.

They reached the corner of the street and lingered a little longer. Then, eventually, they split up, knowing full well that they would meet again in a few days' time, for they all lived in the same district.

As soon as Alison reached home she knew something was wrong. The house seemed strangely still. Even her cat looked forlorn.

"What is the matter, Tinker?" she said as she fumbled for her key. Why was it always at the very bottom of her school bag?

She opened the door, picked Tinker up under her

arm, and stepped into the hall. She didn't call out as she usually did. Something was wrong. Slowly, she put Tinker down, threw her things over the banisters and mounted the stairs. The door of her mother's bedroom was open a little.

"Mum?" she whispered. "Mum?"

There was no reply. Fearfully, she pushed the door. It opened slowly. Then, taking a deep breath, she crept into the room. Immediately, her hand went to her mouth and she swallowed a weak scream. Her mother was lying in the bed. Her eyes were shut. She looked very, very ill.

"Mum?" Alison questioned, nervously.

There was still no answer, not even the faint stirring of a limb, the flicker of an eyelid.

Alison staggered from the room in a daze and stumbled down the stairs. She knew what to do and she must do it at once. There wasn't a moment to lose! The telephone was in the hall. For a minute she couldn't think of their doctor's name but, suddenly, her brain cleared and she flicked through the pages of the directory with expert fingers. Then she lifted the receiver and dialled the number. There was a long pause, an anxious silence, which seemed never ending. Then, with reassuring calm, the doctor's voice sounded in her ear.

"Dr Roberts," he said, abruptly.

His voice was urgent but unhurried; kind but direct. His time was very precious.

"It's Alison Bennett here," she said. "Can you come right away, please? My mother is very ill. She is lying in the bed and I can't wake her."

"Is anybody else in the house?"

"No, doctor. My father is away."

"Don't worry, Alison. I shall be along in two minutes. You live at number seven, don't you?"

"Yes. That's right, doctor. Number seven. Please hurry!"

But the doctor had already replaced his receiver. He was on his way!

Alison went back upstairs. She felt a little less weak now that she knew help was near at hand. But she wanted to see her mother move. She sat by the bed and pulled the covers closer around her mother's chin. Then she felt underneath for her mother's hand and squeezed it.

"It's Alison, Mum," she said, tenderly, hoping that she would be rewarded by a reply. Then she leaned forward and whispered into her mother's ear.

"It's Alison. The doctor will be here in a minute."

The tired eyelids flickered, but they did not open. Alison fancied that her mother had tried to speak. At that moment, a car sped down the road. Alison left the bedside and ran downstairs. She flung open the door and Dr Roberts strode through. He mounted the stairs two at a time, not pausing to speak to her. She didn't know whether to follow him into the bedroom or not, so she waited on the landing in case he needed her. He didn't. After five minutes he emerged. Alison looked up, an unspoken question on her face.

The doctor smiled.

"I think your mother will be all right," he said, warmly. "She needs hospital treatment right away, and a lot of rest. I must telephone for an ambulance. The sooner she is in intensive care, the better,"

"Can I see her now? Is she awake?"

"She is still semi-conscious, Alison. You shouldn't talk to her, but do go and sit with her. She may realise you are there, and that will be a comfort."

Alison went back into the bedroom while the doctor telephoned. Presently, he returned.

"The ambulance is on the way," he said, quietly. "Your mother is going to the main hospital. She will be well looked after there."

Alison smiled for the first time since she had entered the house. She felt as if a great load had been lifted from her shoulders. Her mother was ill, very ill, but she was still alive! Alison had thought her dead. She shuddered at the thought and an icy chill seemed to grip her. The doctor noticed.

"I think you should have a hot drink, young lady," he said.

But the ambulance arrived before the hot drink was prepared and, after the doctor had given precise instructions to the attendants, Alison's mother was lifted gently off the bed on to a stretcher. Alison helped tuck the blankets closely around her. Then, carefully, the stretcher was borne over the banisters and down the stairs. The attendants were competent and kind.

"May I go with her?" Alison asked.

Dr Roberts shook his head.

"It is better that you should stay here," he replied, wisely. "You may be able to visit your mother tomorrow afternoon if she makes good progress. I expect she will fell a little better by then."

One of the attendants stayed in the back of the ambulance with Alison's mother, to attend to her needs on the short journey to the hospital.

They watched as the other man closed the doors quietly.

"Don't worry, dear," he called across to Alison. "We shall soon have your mother safely tucked up in bed. The quiet rest will do her the world of good."

Alison smiled.

"Thanks," she said. "I know you will take good care of her."

The ambulance drove away, smoothly. Alison and the doctor watched until it disappeared around the corner at the far end of the street. Then he led her indoors.

"Now you must have that drink, Alison," he insisted.

The drink was soon prepared and the doctor made her sit down while she sipped it. It warmed her and tasted good.

"I feel better already," she admitted. "Thank you for all your help."

"I haven't finished yet," Dr Roberts replied. "We must contact your father. He will want to see your mother immediately."

"I wish you could," Alison sighed. "He isn't at

the office and I doubt if his company will know where he is exactly."

The doctor looked puzzled.

"He is somewhere in South America," she continued. "He's on a survey in the interior. I suppose he could be contacted by cable and then by radio. We could find out the address of the office in Brazil."

"That is very awkward," Dr Roberts said. "When is your father due to come home?"

"Not for another fortnight. Anyway, it would take him at least three days to get here now. Mother may be much better by then."

The doctor nodded.

"And it is an important survey?" he asked.

"They wouldn't send anyone but my father," she said, rather proudly. "Although Dad wouldn't admit it," she added, hastily.

Dr Roberts laughed.

"I can see you are very fond of your parents," he said. "I think it best to wait until tomorrow before taking any action. We shall have better news for your father then. As you say, he couldn't get here very quickly, even if his company were able to locate him at once."

"He may be miles from any airstrip by now," Alison continued. "And it would be nice to send him good news, wouldn't it?"

"All right, then," the doctor said, rising to his feet. "Will you be able to manage on your own? You have a younger brother, I believe."

"Oh, I can look after Timothy all right. I'm

fourteen, you know! This is the first day of my holidays, so I won't have to miss school. Tim doesn't start his school holidays until Thursday."

"Have you any relatives living in London?"

"No. They are all in the north. And they all have their own children to care for."

The doctor still looked concerned.

"The neighbours are very good," Alison added. "I'm sure they will lend a hand if I really need help."

"You mean the people who were peeping round their curtains just now," Dr Roberts said, smiling. "Yes. They will help. They'll be knocking at your door as soon as I drive away!"

"Aren't neighbours the same everywhere?" Alison asked.

"I suppose so. But I must go now. Break the news gently to young Timothy. I'll telephone you later this evening, when I have been to the hospital to find out how your mother is progressing."

Alison got up and saw the doctor to the front door.

"Thank you so much for all you have done," she said from her heart.

"All part of the service, young lady," he said, cheerfully. "Don't worry, and look after your brother."

Before the doctor had driven the length of the street, the neighbour began to call. Alison was kept busy for the rest of the afternoon. And there were so many things she wanted to do! The neighbours were kind and they would have taken charge of everything. Mrs Green would cook. Mrs Smith would wash the clothes in her up-to-date machine. Mrs Jones would do the ironing. Mrs Brown could send her husband to the shops because he was retired from work and had nothing else to do. They would all visit Alison's mother, of course. And could they go this evening?

Alison felt as if she could scream. The shock of finding her mother had not been a light one and she still felt rather shaky. Besides, Timothy would be home from school. She had to explain to him and she needed to think carefully about what she should say. Timothy was young. He was bound to be very upset. So she set about the task of getting rid of all her neighbours. It wasn't easy, and, afterwards, thinking back, she was sure that she had appeared to be very ungrateful and rather rude. But Timothy!

"Thank you all for being so kind," she said, pushing her way through the small crowd to the front door. "If I need anything, I won't hesitate to call."

The neighbours seemed not to notice. They were busy talking to each other about ailments they had experienced. Alison looked desperate. She coughed loudly, opened the door and rang the bell. The ding-dong chimes were right next to Mrs Smith's ear.

"Oh!" she cried. "You did make me jump! What did you do that for, Alison?" She was rather cross.

"I'm sorry," Alison apologised. "You were all so busy talking, I couldn't make myself heard. Tim will be home in a minute. I must ask you to go."

Mrs Green understood.

"Yes, of course, Alison. We understand."

She pushed her friends along the hall, through the open door, down the garden path and into the street.

Alison sighed, gratefully.

"Thank you, Mrs Green," she said to herself.

Then, Timothy arrived.

CHAPTER TWO

TIMOTHY ASKS SOME QUESTIONS

"Where's Mum?"

Alison smiled.

"Hello, Tim," she said. "Come on inside."

Timothy stepped into the hall and dropped his satchel on the floor. Then, neglecting to remove his shoes as he had been taught, he ran into the kitchen to get a glass of water. It was a very hot day.

Alison stayed in the hall. She hung his satchel in the cupboard and found his slippers. She knew he would be back in a minute. Back with his question. Even now, he was in the garden, perhaps looking in the summer-house to see if his mother was in there. Soon, he reappeared at the kitchen door. Alison looked at his grubby face and at his socks, which were hanging around his ankles. His hands were dirty, too, and his shirt-tail was visible below his school blazer.

"You look disgusting!" she said, gently. "Why don't you clean yourself up before you leave school? You must go into the bathroom and have a jolly good wash. Hang your blazer in the cupboard and put your slippers on. I'll try and find some cool, clean clothes for you."

Timothy looked at her.

"Why you?" he asked. "Where's Mum?"

Alison sighed.

"She isn't very well, Tim," she admitted.

"I'll go up and see her, then," he replied, mounting the stairs before she could stop him.

She followed him as she had followed the doctor a long half hour ago. Timothy came out of the bedroom slowly. All his bounce had gone.

"Where is she?" he asked.

Alison noticed that his eyes were full of tears.

"Mum has gone to hospital," she explained. "But she will be all right. Dr Roberts said so."

Timothy looked doubtful.

"Dr Roberts said I wouldn't get the measles twice. And I did!" Timothy was rather proud of this fact. "Doctors aren't always right, you know."

Alison couldn't help but laugh.

"Into the bathroom!" she said. "I'm sure the doctor will be right this time."

Timothy nodded.

"I expect so," he agreed. "I suppose I was a special case."

He ran the water and, when the basin was almost full, turned off the taps. He put his arms in the water up to his elbows and played with the soap.

"Will Mum be away for long?" he called.

Alison was in his bedroom searching for his clothes.

"Will she be back before my birthday?"

"I expect so."

Alison was turning out his chest of drawers.

"What have you done with your sports shirt?" she called.

He stopped playing with the soap and began to wash.

"I think it's in the linen basket, waiting to be washed," he said.

Alison found another suitable shirt.

"Who will do the washing?"

Timothy had left the bathroom and was standing at his bedroom door. His hands were dripping water everywhere and he still hadn't washed his face.

Alison turned.

"Oh, Timothy!" she said, in despair.

She always called him by his full name when she was displeased.

"Oh, Timothy! Now, go back to the bathroom and don't come out again until you are properly washed and dried. I'll leave your clean things on your bed."

She paused for breath.

"And I shall do the washing, of course!" she added, answering his question at last.

Timothy grinned.

"Deputy Mum," he said.

Deputy was a word he had learned from the television.

Alison chased him back to the bathroom and he slammed the door in her face.

"Mind you are not too long; otherwise I shall eat all your tea," she warned, playfully.

Fortunately, her mother kept a well-stocked larder. Alison opened the refrigerator and searched in the salad drawer. It was that sort of day. A salad day! There was lettuce to wash, tomatoes to slice, beetroot to peel, cucumber, spring onions and red radishes. Timothy loved radishes. She would do a nice lot of those. There was ham and breakfast sausage.

"I wonder why they call it breakfast sausage," she said, half aloud.

She always enjoyed it at tea-time. Her father always said that she liked the right foods at the wrong time.

Timothy came down before tea was quite ready, so he helped to set the table, and took from Alison the things which she passed through the serving hatch. He intended to be helpful and to do his full share of the jobs which needed to be done. After all, he was nearly seven, and he didn't see why Alison should do all the exciting things Mum always did.

"I shall do the washing," he announced, during tea.

Alison spluttered in her cup.

"Don't say funny things when I'm drinking my tea," she said, when she had recovered.

Timothy looked hurt.

"I don't think it's funny," he replied. "The washing has to be done and I shall do it. You have homework to do."

Alison shook her head.

"No, I haven't," she said, firmly. "I'm on holiday."

"That's not fair!" he exclaimed. "If you were still at school you would be glad of somebody like me to do the work for you. Just because you've got all day to do nothing in!"

Alison suddenly felt sorry for him. Of course he wanted to help! She thought hard for a minute.

"I know," she said; "we can do the washing together. Do you know where that apron is that I made you?"

"It's somewhere or other."

Timothy didn't like wearing aprons.

"All right, then. After tea, while I'm washing the dishes, you can find your apron, put it on and clean your shoes for tomorrow. Then we shall do the washing."

"Together!" he said.

They made a splendid job of it. Alison had often helped her mother. She knew which articles to put into the machine first. She knew that she mustn't mix whites with the coloureds. She knew just the right quantity of soap powder needed. In fact, she would have made a first class job of the whole operation. Except for Timothy!

"There!" she said, proudly. "The last load for the spin-drier. I'll peg out some of the other things while the drier is spinning round. Will you carry the basket for me?"

"Yes."

Timothy picked up the basket and the peg bag. There wasn't a lot of room in the kitchen and, as he followed his sister into the garden, he knocked the bowl away from the spin drier. The bowl was there to catch the water which was being wrung from the wet clothes. By the time they returned to the kitchen the drier had done its work. And the kitchen floor was awash!

"Oh, no!"

Alison surveyed the scene sorrowfully.

Timothy was more optimistic.

"Won't take a minute to clear up. Not much mess there."

But it did. By the time they had found clothes and bowls and wheeled out all the other items of equipment, then wheeled them back again, a full half hour had passed. Alison was just straightening her back, when the doorbell rang. It was Mrs Smith.

"I've come for the washing," she said. "It's a nice fine evening for drying, too."

Alison looked guilty. How could she explain? "Well, actually, Mrs Smith, I've done it. There wasn't much, and Tim wanted to help. In fact, he wanted to do it on his own."

Alison hoped she would understand.

"But I said I would do it for you," Mrs Smith protested.

"I know."

Alison tried to soothe her.

"I know you did, Mrs Smith, and I really am grateful. I'm sure there will be a lot more washing to do if Mum has to stay in hospital for long. I shall be glad of your help. It's Tim, you see. He misses Mum and he does want to help me as much as he can."

Mrs Smith's face softened.

"All right, Alison. But, remember, you have only to ask and I'll come over to help you whenever I can. I hope your mother will get along nicely. Is there any more news?"

"No. There isn't yet. I am expecting the doctor to telephone later this evening. He was going in to the hospital after surgery finished."

Just then Timothy appeared in the hall.

"Hello, Mrs Smith," he said, mischievously. "I've just done the washing."

Alison looked at him sternly.

"Well," he continued. "Alison did help a little."

"What did she want?" Timothy asked, rather rudely, when Mrs Smith had gone. "Can't she see we can manage between us?"

"Shoosh, Timothy!" Alison scolded. "I expect we shall have a lot of visits from the neighbours. It's good of them to want to help. There may be many things we can't manage on our own."

When they returned to the kitchen, Tinker came in from the garden.

"It's time for his tea now," Timothy said. "That is one job I can do without any help. Just leave him to me."

All through the early evening the kind neighbours called. One of them brought a cake she had baked, and it was still warm from the oven. Alison had difficulty in preventing Timothy from having a slice.

"You had your tea only two hours ago," she insisted. "We must carry on just the same as if Mum were here."

Then, for some time, there was a complete lull in the calls. The evening wore on and the expected telephone message didn't arrive. Alison wondered whether she should ring the doctor to find out how her mother was progressing, but he had promised to let her know and she felt sure he would keep his word. When the sun began to sink low below the rooftops, Alison decided that it was time for Timothy to go to bed. Indeed, it was long past his normal bedtime.

"You have to go to school tomorrow," she said, brushing aside all his protests.

She gave him a drink and ushered him up the stairs to his room.

"You'll have to read to me this evening," he said.

Timothy loved to hear a story before he went to sleep. Alison picked up the book.

"But you had this one read to you a fortnight ago," she said.

Timothy nodded.

"That's right. Mum has read it twice to me already. It's my favourite. That's why. Haven't you a favourite book?"

Alison smiled. She remembered when she was Tim's age how her parents had taken turns to read to her and how much she had enjoyed it.

"All right," she said. "Just ten minutes. Then you really must go to sleep."

Timothy listened attentively without interrupting. Then, when Alison closed the book, he spoke.

"Do you think God will make Mum well again?" he asked.

Alison stroked his brow.

"Yes. I do," she replied.

He still looked worried.

"Why didn't He stop her being ill?"

Questions! Alison didn't know quite what to say.

"I don't know, Tim," she said at last. "I don't know all the answers. But there is a verse in the Bible that says all things work together for good to those that love God."

"And Mum loves God!"

Timothy smiled.

"Yes. Mum loves God. Do you?"

Timothy didn't answer.

"I'll ask Him to be sure to make Mum better quickly," he said, ignoring her direct question. "Perhaps He will send her back home tomorrow."

"Perhaps He thinks it better for Mum to have a nice, quiet rest in hospital," Alison observed.

"Then I shall tell Him that Mum likes it best at home," he replied.

Alison laughed.

"Then ask Him nicely," she said, pulling the curtains. "And I shall ask Him, too."

Later, when she was taking the last few items of laundry off the line, she glanced up at Timothy's window. He was peeping round the curtains. She pretended not to notice. The washing was nicely dry, and, when she had folded the clothes, she thought of starting the ironing, but it was already late. She wondered whether to do just a little, when her mind was made up for her. Somebody was at the door. It was Dr Roberts.

"Sorry I'm so late," he apologised. "But what is so dangerous about this house?"

Alison looked puzzled.

"This notice was pinned to your front door," the doctor said, showing her a scrap of paper torn from an exercise book.

"Danger. Keep out!"

Alison read the notice and blushed crimson.

"That is my brother's way of protecting me from the neighbours," she said. "I wondered why we hadn't had any callers for the last two hours!"

"It seems to have worked well," the doctor replied. "Children can do outrageous things and get away with them, sometimes, especially if they are very young. I'm sure you wouldn't have dared to do anything like that!"

"How is my mother?"

Alison wanted to stop talking about frivolous things.

The doctor looked serious again.

"She is as well as can be expected, but she is quite seriously ill. I am glad to say she has responded to treatment and she is now fully conscious. And she asked after you."

"Will I be able to see her tomorrow?"

"I think so, if you stay for a little while, Alison; but the ward sister will decide that."

"Will my mother be in hospital for long?"

The doctor looked thoughtful.

"That is rather difficult to say. I think she has a good chance of coming home in about two weeks.

Your father will be home long before then."

Alison sighed.

"Yes. I wish he were here now, not because we can't manage, but for Mum's sake. Should we contact him right away, do you think?"

"It's too late to do that today," Dr Roberts said. "And you look as if you need a good night's rest. Here, take this tablet in a glass of water before you lie down. It will help you to sleep soundly. You will feel much better in the morning. I must be on my way home now."

"Thank you for calling again," she said, gratefully. "I am so glad my mother will not be away for too long. Although, a fortnight!"

"Take each day as it comes, Alison. You will manage, I know."

The doctor's tone was reassuring.

"Goodnight, Alison. All will be well."

When he had gone, Alison left the ironing and went straight upstairs. She peeped at Timothy, who was fast asleep. He had thrown back the covers and she drew them around him, in case he should feel cold in the night. Then, she went to her own room.

CHAPTER THREE

A TESTING TIME

Sleep did not come easily to Alison that night in spite of the sedative she had been given. Although she was a Christian and trusted in God's fatherly care, she could not help feeling anxious about her mother, for she had looked very ill indeed. Alison wondered whether the doctor was trying to be kind in being more optimistic than he ought to be. This was the first big crisis she had faced since handing over control of her life to the Lord Jesus Christ some six months ago. She had not yet fully proved that her Lord was everything He claimed to be for her, better even than father and mother put together.

She listened to the regular ticking of her alarm clock. Twice she switched on her bedside lamp and stared at the yellow light for a while to try to make her eyes tired, but she only made them hurt and, when she switched off the lamp, she was glad of the darkness again. At about one o'clock, she slipped off into an uneasy sleep. An hour or so later, she was awakened by a cry. Tim!

She rubbed her sleepy eyes and stumbled out of bed. She didn't bother to grope for her dressing-gown but ran across the landing to his room. He was sitting up in bed.

"What's the matter, Tim?" she asked, tenderly,

putting her arm round his hot shoulders.

"I've been dreaming," he said, beginning to cry again.

"Everything is all right, Tim," she said. "I'm here now. It was only a dream."

Tim's eyes were wide. He had had quite a fright.

"Can I have a drink of water?"

"Of course you can! I'll run along to the bathroom and get one for you."

She left the room.

"Poor old Tim!" she thought. "So he was worried, too."

She hurried back and he took the beaker from her and gulped the cold water.

"That's better," he said, when he had finished. "Can I have some more?"

Alison laughed.

"I suppose so," she said. "But too much isn't good for you."

"It's better with the light on," Timothy said, when he had downed the second beaker full. "I had a most horrid dream!"

"You will feel better now," she replied, trying to console him. "I'll shake up your pillow and tidy your bed. That will make you feel cooler."

Timothy jumped out of bed and watched his sister.

"Do you think God will make Mum better?" he enquired.

"Is that what you dreamt about?"

Timothy nodded.

He jumped back into bed and Alison stroked his forehead as he lay back on the pillow.

"Did you ask God to make Mum better?" she asked.

He nodded again.

"Then He will!"

Timothy looked doubtful.

"He might not. I haven't always been good. He might not listen to me."

Alison smiled again.

"Then God wouldn't answer anybody's prayers," she said. "We have all done wrong and we all need His forgiveness."

"Even Dad?"

Timothy's eyes were bright and moist.

"Of course!"

He looked relieved.

"God always hears our prayers when we mean what we say," she continued. "He loves to forgive us and to take our sins away. That's why He sent the Lord Jesus to die on the cross, to save us from our sins. But God won't take our badness away until we know we are bad and we ask Him to."

"Is that all we have to do?"

"Nearly all, Tim. But we have to mean what we say and we have to make up our minds to turn away from bad things and to follow the Lord Jesus. He helps us to do this. We can't do it on our own."

Timothy looked relieved.

"He must be a very nice person," he said.

Alison kissed him and he snuggled down under

the bedclothes in his own private little world.

"I'll leave the door open if you promise to go straight to sleep," she said.

"I promise," he yawned.

He was almost too tired to speak. Alison crept out of the room back to her own bed. In a very few minutes she was asleep, too.

Her alarm clock rang at the appointed time in the morning but she didn't hear it. The sedative given by the doctor had taken effect and, for the latter part of the night at least, she had slept soundly. She would have slept on and on and on, but for Timothy. Dreamily, she was half aware of somebody tugging at her bedclothes. She wrapped them closer.

"Oh, wake up, Alison!"

Timothy was desperate.

"Wake up!"

Alison stirred and opened one eye. Timothy was a blurred little boy at the foot of her bed.

"It's you!" she said. "What is the matter now?"

"It's morning, Alison!"

But the only reply he received was a deep grunt. The only movement Alison made was to turn away from him and to face the wall.

"Go back to bed," she moaned.

Timothy sighed. Then he smiled. He knew how to wake his sister. Lightly, in his bare feet, he tripped along to the bathroom and picked up a flannel. He soaked it in cold water and then ran back. The surplus water ran through his eager fingers on to the floor. Deftly, he pulled the covers back from

Alison's face and plonked the soggy flannel on her nose. She shot up straight and flung the flannel to the furthest corner of the room. Timothy put his hand to his mouth and made funny noises. He didn't dare laugh properly.

"Couldn't you see I was having a nice sleep?" she complained, bitterly. "What's the time, anyway?"

"Eight o'clock," Timothy said, still trying to suppress his merriment. "And I shall be late for school."

"Oh dear!" she sighed. "I meant to be up early! Hurry up and dress while I see to your breakfast."

Timothy went back to his room and, when he had made quite sure the door was closed safely behind him, he collapsed into uncontrollable laughter. Alison, in her room, heard him rolling over his bed, and she couldn't help laughing, too. She put on her dressing-gown, retrieved the flannel from where she had flung it and took it back to the bathroom.

"Breakfast in five minutes," she called, as she ran downstairs. "Mind you put your tie on properly this morning."

But Timothy hardly heard. He was still laughing.

Timothy had to be content with a cold breakfast. There wasn't time to cook anything; he would have been late for school.

"Aren't you having any?" he asked.

Alison looked through the serving hatch.

"Don't speak with your mouth full of cornflakes," she teased.

Timothy screwed up his nose.

"You haven't answered my question," he persisted.

"I'll have some later," she said, yawning widely and stretching her arms above her head. "I am so tired!"

"Good job you haven't got to go to school like I have!" Timothy retorted. "Trouble with girls is they can never get up in the morning!"

Timothy didn't know about the sedative. He didn't mean to be unkind.

"Can I mash my banana this morning, please?" he asked, when he had finished his cereal. "Mum lets me put milk and sugar on it, too."

Alison sighed.

"Oh, all right," she said, "if you must make such a mess with your food. Here, take this fork. You'll find the milk and sugar on the table."

"There's no need to be crotchety," he said.

It wasn't one of Alison's best mornings, so she stayed in the kitchen and fiddled with some odds and ends. When Timothy had finished eating, he came out to her.

"Will you be going to see Mum this afternoon?" he enquired.

Alison looked down at his earnest face, straightened his tie, and smiled.

"I hope so," she said. "Dr Roberts is going to let me know this morning."

Timothy rinsed his hands at the kitchen sink and dried them slowly on a towel. Alison watched him. She knew he was about to ask another awkward question.

"Can I come?"

Alison shook her head.

"I wish you could," she replied. "But you have to go to school. Besides, you are not old enough."

He walked out into the garden without a word. She watched him, hoping she hadn't hurt him. He wasn't old enough, it was true, but she shouldn't have said so. How she wished her mother were here to deal with him! She would know what to say and how to say it. That was important, too.

Presently, Timothy came back.

"Will you take these for Mum?" he asked, holding out a handful of small flowers he had picked from his own special patch in the garden.

"Oh, they are beautiful!" Alison exclaimed. "Mum will love those, especially as you grew them."

She looked around the kitchen for a piece of tissue paper which had been wrapped around a loaf of bread.

"Here," she said, smoothing it carefully. "Let's wrap them up in this, like they do at the florist's."

When they had finished. Timothy felt better.

"I'll go and pack my satchel," he said. "Can you give me some money to pay for my school dinner?"

Alison had quite forgotten that she would need money. She doubted if she had enough in her room to pay for the shopping she would have to do. But she found some money for Timothy's meal and added a little extra for him to buy some sweets to help him to forget his disappointment at not being old enough to visit his mother.

"There," she said, ever so gently. "When you come home I shall be able to tell you how Mum is. And I'll be sure to take your flowers."

She watched him run off down the street and she was glad when one of his friends joined him. She closed the front door and went back to the kitchen. Now she would eat her own breakfast!

During the morning Mrs Jones called. Alison had just finished making the beds and tidying the house.

"I won't hinder you, dear," the good neighbour said.

"That's all right," Alison replied, trying to make amends for her somewhat impolite conduct of the previous evening.

"I have just come from the surgery," Mrs Jones continued. "My husband needed some more medicine and, unless I made the effort to call in to see the doctor, he wouldn't bother to collect it. He hates taking medicine!"

Alison smiled.

"Did Dr Roberts give you any message for me?"

"Yes. He says it will be all right for you to see your mother this afternoon, after two o'clock. Just for a little while. The ward sister will be expecting you."

"Did he say how Mum is?"

"No, dear, he didn't, but I expect she is making progress; otherwise they wouldn't be too happy about you visiting her."

"That is true," Alison agreed. "I must hurry with

the other jobs before this afternoon. I mustn't be late!"

Mrs Jones laughed.

"I can see your mother has trained you well. I saw all your washing on the line last night. Why don't you let me iron it for you? I haven't very much to do this afternoon."

"Oh, would you really?" Alison said, gratefully. "I'm not very good at ironing. Mum always does it for us."

"Then I'll take it now."

Alison put all the ironing into a big plastic bag and handed it to her neighbour.

"It's very kind of you," she said. "I shall tell Mum that Tim and I are being well cared for while she's away."

"That's right. I expect she will worry about you, with your father being away as well. But we'll keep an eye on you."

Alison laughed. Her conversation with Mrs Jones was making her feel much happier.

"I'll give Mum your love," she said.

Alison went to the shops before lunch. She needed bread and vegetables, besides other things. When she was in the supermarket she bumped into one of her school friends.

"Hello, Alison. So you are running errands, too!"

Jill was a tall, blonde-haired girl with an infectious grin.

"Hello, Jill. Yes. I'm the head cook and bottle-washer, as well!"

Jill grimaced.

"Is your mother on strike?" she joked.

Alison chose her vegetables.

"No. Mum is in hospital."

Jill's cheerful face clouded.

"I am sorry! Did she expect to? You didn't mention it at school."

Jill dropped a lettuce in her basket.

"Mum had a heart attack," Alison said. "I'm going to see her this afternoon."

Jill looked alarmed.

"I say, I'm awfully sorry," she repeated. "Is there anything I can do to help?"

"That is kind of you," Alison replied. "You know, since last night, people have been so kind. I think I can manage until Dad arrives home. Then he can take charge!"

They paid for their purchases at the checkout and stepped into the street.

"But isn't your father in America? Will he be home in time?"

Alison looked shocked.

"My mother isn't that seriously ill," she said, taken aback by her friend's remark.

Jill shook her head vigorously.

"No, silly! I didn't mean that! What about your holiday? Will you be able to go?"

A sudden dawning of truth surged through Alison. She had forgotten all about her holiday! Events had moved so quickly she had hardly had time to think.

"My holiday!" she said, weakly. "I had forgotten all about it!"

"You must go, Alison! You must!"

Jill was definite.

"I don't see how I can," Alison protested. "I couldn't go and leave Mum when she is so ill, could I?"

"But you won it! It just isn't fair!"

Alison smiled.

"Don't get upset about it," she said. "Perhaps I am meant to stay in England."

Jill snorted.

"And everything will work out in the end," she said, rather unkindly. "Well! If you can believe that, you can believe anything! How can you stand there and imply that God is in control of things when everything goes wrong?"

Alison looked sad. Jill knew she was a Christian.

"It is nice of you to be so concerned," she replied. "I wish I could explain to you. It is so difficult to put into words, but I have asked God to direct my life in every detail. I'm not risking anything by handing my life over to Him. He sees the future as easily as we see the past. I couldn't be in safer hands. I trusted Him to take away my sins. Surely it isn't too much for Him to do something far less, to deal with this present situation? He will never let me down. He always means what He says, and He is well able to do what He means!"

Jill smiled.

"It must be nice to be a Christian, but I only

believe what I can see," she said, more gently. "But, honestly, I do hope you are right and things do work out in the end. It would be such a pity not to go to Kenya."

As Alison walked home she couldn't help but think about what her friend had said. Yes, it would be a pity, but there were more important things than holidays. But, when she reached home and opened the door, a letter was lying on the door-mat. It was big and glossy. She picked it up and turned it over. It was her final instructions for the safari trip she had earned. Limply, she sat down on the stairs and buried her face in her hands. It wasn't always easy to be a Christian.

CHAPTER FOUR

THE VISIT

Alison didn't allow herself to feel depressed for long. As the morning passed, she became more and more excited at the prospect of seeing her mother again. Was it only yesterday when illness had struck as suddenly as lightning? It seemed a lifetime ago! She had lunch early and then busied herself preparing for the visit. She spent a long time deciding what to wear and, more than once, changed her mind. In the end, she chose her best outfit. She brushed her long, brown hair carefully and toyed with half a dozen unnecessary things before looking at her watch again. It was only one o'clock. She wished she hadn't eaten her lunch so early.

Suddenly, she decided she couldn't bear to wait any longer. She felt she just had to leave the house. She went down to the kitchen to rewrap Timothy's flowers which she had stood in water to keep them fresh. Then she picked up her handbag and walked out into the afternoon sunshine.

One of the neighbours was doing some work in her front garden. She paused and looked up.

"Give your mother my love," she called, when she saw Alison.

Alison smiled.

"Thank you, I will," she replied.

The neighbour watched as Alison walked by.

"My! You do look smart today!" she said, half aloud.

But Alison didn't hear.

The hospital was a short bus ride away but, in order to use a little more time, Alison walked. Presently, she came to a quiet residential area and she saw the huge block of hospital buildings in the distance. An ambulance rushed by and she caught her breath. Quickly, she breathed a silent prayer for whoever was inside the vehicle. She hadn't thought very much about sick people until now.

A cheery porter stood outside his office by the huge iron gates which guarded the entrance to the hospital grounds.

"You are nice and early," he said, pleasantly.

Alison looked at her watch again.

"It is nearly twenty minutes to two," she protested.

The porter laughed.

"You look as if you just can't wait a second to get inside the hospital," he replied. "Tell me. Is it your boy friend you have come to visit?"

Alison blushed.

"No, it isn't! I've come to see my mother. She came in yesterday."

The porter became more serious.

"Then you may not know which ward she is in. Look. Do you see that building over there?"

He pointed in the direction he wanted her to go.

Alison shaded her eyes from the sun.

"Yes," she said. "There is a blue door in the middle of the block."

"That's the one. If you go in that door you will see another door marked 'Almoner's Office'. Go straight in and they will be able to direct you."

Alison thanked him.

"I hope your mother is improving," he called, as she hurried off to see the almoner.

A secretary sat at a desk in the office and she looked up when Alison entered the room.

"Can I help you?" she asked.

"I have come to visit my mother, but I'm not sure which ward she's in. The porter said you would be able to tell me."

The secretary smiled.

"Yes," she said. "We can tell you. What is your mother's name and when was she admitted?"

Alison told her and watched as the secretary thumbed through a box of index cards.

"Here we are. Ward B3. You walk out of this building, turn right, right again, and then it is the second block on the left. Ward B3 is on the third floor. You can't miss it!"

Alison wasn't so sure! She thanked the secretary and hurried away before she forgot the directions. It was near to the visiting hour and she didn't want to be late. That would never do! She reached the entrance to the ward just in time to see a group of visitors being admitted early to see their relatives. She was about to follow, when a nurse stopped her.

"Who do you wish to see?"

Her manner was not unkind, but very firm.

"My mother."

Alison felt anxious now.

"Mrs Bennett," she added, realising that the nurse would want to know the name.

"You must be her daughter," the nurse replied, putting Alison more at ease.

Alison nodded.

"May I see my mother, please? How is she?" she asked.

"You may see her in a few minutes, but the ward sister wants to have a word with you first. You had better wait in here. Sister won't be long."

The nurse pushed the glass door of a side room and invited Alison to sit and wait. A few magazines were scattered on a small table which stood in the centre of the room. The walls were painted cream and were well scrubbed. Apart from three chairs and the table, the room was bare. The floor was uncarpeted.

Alison sat down. She felt very uneasy. Why had the nurse let the other visitors in and kept her out? Had her mother's condition grown worse? She remembered that the nurse hadn't answered her enquiry as to how her mother was. She looked at her watch again. It was already ten minutes after the proper time for visiting. Her mother would imagine Alison hadn't bothered to come. Suddenly, she felt very miserable.

While Alison waited in silence, she listened to the sounds of other people's activity. She wished she could be busy, also. She heard a trolley being pushed along, then a whirr of machinery. She guessed this noise was made by a lift. Two doctors paused for a while outside her door, and she saw through the frosted glass that they were engaged in quiet conversation. Yes! This is the real world, she thought. A world where lives were saved and lost. A battleground. A world of planned efficiency and ordered activity. A world which, up to now, she had thought of so rarely. Then the door opened. The ward sister had arrived at last!

"Hello, Alison. I'm sorry you have had to wait so long."

Alison wondered how the sister knew her name, but thought that Dr Roberts must have told her.

"May I see my mother, please?"

Her questions were becoming as direct as Timothy's!

"Yes, of course. I'll take you to her right away. We have put your mother in a little ward where she has special attention. She will be so pleased to see you."

Alison followed her out of the room and down the corridor. She wished the sister would hurry and, when a nurse stopped to ask a question, Alison felt she would simply burst with frustration.

"We don't hurry here," the sister said, when she had answered the query. "There are many needs to be attended to in a large hospital."

Alison took heed of the rebuke. True, she was very anxious about her own mother, but there were other people's mothers, and fathers, too; all sorts of people with all sorts of needs. She made up her mind to try to be patient.

The little ward contained two beds, which were both screened from view by floral curtains. It was impossible for Alison to tell which bed contained her mother.

"I'll leave you for ten minutes," the sister whispered. "Don't worry about all the equipment or anything else you see. It's all for your mother's benefit, and she is doing very nicely."

The sister pointed to the bed on the left and pushed Alison gently forward.

"Your mother is over there," she said, quietly.

In contrast to the previous time of waiting, the ten minutes Alison spent with her mother seemed like seconds. When the sister returned, long before Alison said half of what she wanted to say, she could hardly believe that her time was up.

"But you said ten minutes!" she protested, when she had said goodbye to her mother and was back in the corridor.

"You have had over a quarter of an hour."

The sister led her along to her private office.

"You can come again tomorrow," she said.

But tomorrow was another day.

"We are trying to contact your father through his company," the sister continued. "I am sure he will fly home as soon as he receives the message. Your mother gave us the details, and we thought it best for him to know of her illness without delay."

Alison smiled.

"I hope he won't feel too worried," she said. "I expect it will take him several days to get to London."

"I think we have made it clear that your mother isn't in any danger now," the sister replied.

And with those comforting words ringing in her ears, Alison made her way home. Timothy was waiting for her on the doorstep.

"When is Mum coming home? Tomorrow?"

Alison opened the front door and ushered him inside.

"Not tomorrow," she said.

"Did Mum like my flowers?"

A smile spread across Alison's face.

"She thought they were wonderful!" she exclaimed. "I put them in a pretty little vase and Mum said they were better than all the other flowers in the hospital put together."

Timothy looked pleased and doubtful all at the same time.

"You are just saying that," he replied. "You don't really mean it. They have much better flowers at the florist's. I've seen them."

"Mum thought yours were the best because they came from home."

And that remark made Timothy very pleased.

"Can I have the hose on while you are setting the tea?" he asked, when he had drunk a long, cool drink in the kitchen. "The garden looks as if it needs a drink, too."

"Only if you wear your swimming trunks," Alison warned. "And don't squirt the water through the windows or over the fence."

Timothy bounded upstairs and rummaged in a drawer for his trunks. He was back in next to no time.

"Strange how easily you can find things when you want to," Alison observed.

But Timothy didn't heed her remark. He was already unrolling the hose.

Alison didn't hurry over the preparation of the tea. Once or twice she looked out of the window to make sure Timothy was keeping the spray under control. She smiled when she noticed how wet he was and how his small body glistened in the sun. Water would freshen him after his long, hot day in the classroom, and she didn't bother to remind him that it was the flowers that needed the spray.

After tea the doctor called. She didn't answer the door herself, as she was busy washing the dishes, so she sent Timothy. She heard the doctor's deep, friendly voice and hurriedly dried her hands.

"It's Dr Roberts," Timothy announced from the hall.

Alison led him into the sitting-room.

"I hope I haven't called at an inconvenient time," he said.

Alison laughed.

"We are usually busy," she said. "I didn't realise how much Mum does, until she went away. I haven't done half the jobs she usually does. It isn't as tidy as when Mum is here," she continued, looking around at some of Timothy's things which were scattered on the floor.

The doctor laughed.

"I expect you find it a little difficult to keep everything in the right place, with a young brother like Timothy in the house."

Alison laughed, too. She liked Dr Roberts. He seemed to understand.

"How was your mother this afternoon? I guess she was very pleased to see you."

"Oh, yes! And I was pleased to see her, though the time passed far too quickly. I think Mum was concerned about us being here on our own, but I think I reassured her that she had nothing to worry about. What we can't do ourselves, the neighbours do for us. They are very kind."

Dr Roberts nodded.

"Good," he said. "Your mother seems to be making normal progress now and I think she will be able to come home in a fortnight. That's worth waiting for, isn't it?"

Alison sighed with relief.

"It's nice to hear you say that," she admitted. "I was very worried when I saw all the equipment by the bed. I didn't know they had machines to help patients with bad hearts."

"They have nearly everything these days," the doctor replied. "But patients still need very careful nursing, despite all our modern aids. Your mother is in very good hands. I have known that ward sister for several years. She has the best welfare of her patients always at heart."

There was a brief pause in the conversation and Timothy came in. The doctor ruffled his hair and patted him on the back. Alison knew by the expression on her brother's face that he was going to ask another big question.

"When is my dad coming home?"

The doctor looked serious.

"Do you know, Timothy, that was the very thing I came to talk about. I'm glad you came in when you did."

Timothy looked pleased with himself.

"The sister told me she had contacted his company and they were going to send a cable right away," the doctor said.

"So when will he be home?" Timothy said.

"Ssh, Tim."

Alison tried to restrain him.

"Ssh! He will come home as soon as he can. Dad has to be contacted first. He might be two days' journey from a jungle airstrip. Then he has to wait for a plane to arrive to take him to the main airport. He couldn't possibly be home for another four or five days."

Timothy looked downcast.

"Now, Timothy. You can manage until then, I know," Dr Roberts said, cheerily. "We men know how to look after ourselves, don't we?"

Timothy smiled briefly.

"Of course I can manage!" he said. "I wasn't

thinking about myself. What about Alison's holiday?"

The doctor looked puzzled.

"What is this about, Alison?" he asked.

Alison looked embarrassed.

"Oh, it doesn't matter," she said. "I wouldn't think of going away while Mum is ill. Besides, Timothy—"

"Don't worry about me," Timothy interrupted. "I can sleep at my friend's house. Alison is supposed to be flying to Kenya on Saturday. And it's Wednesday now!"

"Kenya!"

It was the doctor's turn to be surprised.

"Is this true, Alison?"

She admitted that it was. She wished Timothy would keep silent for once.

"Alison won a competition out of thirty thousand people," he explained, proudly. "She is to fly out to Kenya to see all the wild animals in the national parks. She is—"

"Ssh. Timothy," Alison said, putting her hand over his mouth. "It isn't any use trying to persuade me," she continued, firmly. "I can't go!"

CHAPTER FIVE

TIMOTHY TAKES OFF

After the doctor had left and Timothy was in bed, Alison went to her room. She had not opened her letter previously, but now she must not delay reading it. The organisers of the competition she had won would need to know right away that she wouldn't be going. It was a very difficult moment for Alison. Things hadn't worked out as she would have wished, but, in spite of this, she still trusted God. She had asked Him to guide her, and He wouldn't let her down. She fumbled with the letter, which was difficult to open because of the stiff, glossy envelope. She half withdrew the contents and then paused. She sat on her bed, the letter still in her hands, and bowed her head.

"Heavenly Father, You know what this letter contains. You know how much I want to go to Kenya. You know about Mum. You know about Tim. You know where Dad is. Help me to answer this letter. Help me to do what is right in Your sight. Please help me to say no."

Her prayer was direct and simple. That was how she always spoke to God.

The envelope contained wonderful pictures of the national park in East Africa. She read the descriptive guide. 'These are just a few of the animals you will see in their natural state', it began. She screwed her fingers into the palms of her hands in frustration. 'This is the programme for the two weeks. You leave London Airport at...'

Alison got up and tidied her dressing-table. It was quite unnecessary, of course, but she had to do something to take her mind from the letter. It was a fabulous trip! And it wasn't easy to do what was right. Presently, she became calmer, more resolved. Deliberately, she reached for her writing paper, took her pen and began to write the fateful letter. Even before she had finished, she felt a wonderful sense of peace, an assurance that she had done what God wanted her to do. And she knew He had heard her prayer.

She slept soundly, but she awoke in good time to call Timothy for his last day at school. She wanted to give him a nice breakfast; to take her mother's place. She guessed that Timothy missed his mother far more than he cared to admit. And he was unusually quiet this morning.

She listened for the normal sounds from the bathroom above her as she worked in the kitchen. He was quiet! Even the water running down the pipe seemed to be sneaking away before being noticed. Then, suddenly, he appeared at the kitchen door.

"You did make me jump, Tim!" she exclaimed. "I didn't hear you come down the stairs."

Timothy sighed.

"I wish Mum was back," he said.

Alison looked at him intently.

"So you don't think I'm looking after you properly," she said lightly, trying to shake him out of his melancholy mood. "Is that what it is?"

"No, it isn't that," he replied.

But he wouldn't say what it was that troubled him.

All through breakfast, Alison tried to cheer him. It took him three times as long as it usually did to eat his cereal and, even though she prepared him another banana, he ate it without much enthusiasm.

"It's my last day at school today," he reminded her, finally breaking his long silence. "I shall bring home my report and all my paintings."

So that was it. His paintings!

"I'll take the best paintings to the hospital to show Mum," Alison promised. "She will love to see them."

Timothy was very proud of his paintings. He had a very good idea of colour and shapes. They were easily the best in the class. Alison would look at every one closely, because it would please him.

"I'd like to take them to show Mum, myself," he said, after another period of thought. "Yes. I'd like that very much."

Alison's face clouded. She didn't know what to say. She didn't want to upset him.

"I'll ask the ward sister if you can come with me tomorrow," she said. "I promise I will."

Timothy's sad face brightened for a moment and then he looked unhappy again.

"She won't let me come with you," he said. "It's

the rules," he complained. "Why do they have so many rules?"

"I'll try very hard to persuade her," Alison said. "You leave it to me, Tim. I shall do my very best."

And Timothy had to be content with that.

It was still early when they cleared the table, so Timothy helped Alison to dry the dishes and to tidy the room. He seemed not to want to go to school too early, and she had to remind him that the last day of term was usually exciting and he would be sorry if he missed any of it. She gave him her letter to post and, finally, he ran off clutching it in his hand. She watched him go, feeling very uneasy at the strange mood he was in. She thought of following him to school to make sure he arrived safely, but she dismissed the idea immediately. She didn't want to spy on him. She was too fond of him to do that. But her feeling of uneasiness persisted all the morning.

At lunchtime, the telephone rang. Alison ran into the hall.

"Hello."

She held the receiver close to her ear.

"Hello, Alison. It's Miss Formby here. Has Timothy arrived home?"

A shiver shot up Alison's spine.

"No, Miss Formby. He hasn't."

"Well, he seems to have eaten his dinner and left. Perhaps he thought it was a half day."

Miss Formby sounded rather cross.

"I expect he will be here in a minute," Alison said. "He did seem a little upset this morning, and

I think he may be coming home so that he can go to the hospital with me this afternoon."

"How is your mother getting on?"

Miss Formby sounded more sympathetic now.

"Slowly, but well, thank you. But we shall be so glad to have her home. Especially Tim."

"Well, do let me know if he doesn't arrive. If I don't hear from you, I'll presume he has got home safely. And I do hope your mother continues to make progress."

She rang off and Alison replaced the receiver. She went outdoors and looked down the road in the direction Timothy should come. There was no sign of him at all. He ought to be in sight if he intended to come home. She decided to do something active to find him and to still the feeling of dread which she could not suppress inside her. So she ran indoors, grabbed her coat and umbrella, for the sky looked as if it would rain, and quickly left the house. Somehow, somewhere, she must find Tim before she visited her mother. She looked at her watch. She had only an hour and a half. It wasn't really long enough.

She went to Timothy's friend's house first. As she walked, she kept looking round in case he was tracking her. He could be exasperating at times, like most brothers. But there was no sign of him. And he wasn't with his friend. She decided to look in the park.

The park was a small one and the activity was centred on a play area in the middle of the green expanse. Children swung themselves into the air on the swings and twirled around on the roundabouts. Alison hurried across the soft grass to have a closer look and, shielding her eyes from the sun, which peeped through the black clouds, she scanned every inch of the area. Tim wasn't on the swings; he wasn't on the roundabouts; he wasn't among the children queueing to use the slide. He wasn't on the seesaws; he wasn't on the climbing frames. He wasn't anywhere! She was on the point of leaving the central area when she thought of the tunnel. Even as she looked in that direction, she saw a small boy run out and then dash back inside again. Was it Tim? She couldn't be certain. There was only one way to find out.

"I'll have to crawl inside, I suppose," she sighed.

She hurried across and, as quietly as she could, hoping nobody would notice, she bent low and crept through the maze of concrete pipes, which had been provided for the children. The tunnels were short and she looked in all of them. In the last one she found a boy. He wasn't Tim!

"What do you think you're doing in here?" he asked, very rudely. "These tunnels aren't for big girls like you."

Alison blushed. She felt very embarrassed.

"I'm looking for my little brother," she explained.

"Well, he isn't in here."

"So I see," she replied, keeping her head down so as not to scrape the roof of the tunnel.

"There haven't been any boys in here for ages. They're all on the swings."

"Thank you."

Alison made as dignified an exit as possible and crawled along to the far end of the tunnel, dragging her umbrella behind her. She hoped nobody would see her emerge. She was fortunate. The children were being rounded up by their mothers, who wanted to reach home before the storm broke. She breathed another silent prayer. Tim hated thunder!

"Let him be safe," she prayed, as the first big drops of rain sploshed on her head.

She raised her umbrella and made for a row of tall trees which would give her shelter. A flash of lightning slashed the sky, and the roll of thunder, almost immediately, sounded like a giant clearing his throat. The storm was almost directly overhead. She looked back towards the tunnel and thought of the boy inside, but she guessed, rightly, that he wouldn't be very much concerned. He was in the safest placc. She glanced round the park, which had emptied as if by magic. The rain was torrential; the grass was fast becoming a shallow lake. Another flash of lightning split the sky and Alison remembered the tall trees. Gathering her coat around her and using her umbrella to force back the rain, she fled across the soggy ground to the park gates and the safety of a bus shelter. An old lay stood underneath.

"Sudden, wasn't it?" the old lady said.

Alison regained her breath and shook her umbrella.

"Yes. It was."

The old lady eyed her closely.

"You don't mind the storm, do you?" she asked, kindly.

Alison shook her head. She wasn't afraid.

"You are worried about something, my dear. I can tell."

"I was looking for my young brother," Alison admitted. "I thought he might be in the park, but he wasn't. He doesn't like storms."

"I expect he has sheltered somewhere," the old lady said. "Are you waiting for a bus? Look; one is coming up the hill."

Alison peered through the rain. The red bus came nearer, tossing the water off the road as a ship ploughs through the sea. She stuck her hand out and the driver pulled the heavy vehicle to the side of the road, sending the water splashing high up Alison's legs. But she didn't care. She helped the old lady on and then climbed aboard. The bus was going near to the hospital and she might just be there on time. She sat upstairs and noticed that the rain was easing and a broad, bright rainbow straddled the sky. She remembered Noah and God's promise. God was still the same! Five minutes later, the storm went away.

The bus driver didn't seem to be in any hurry. Alison peered through the rain-splashed windows to see what progress they were making. She was not so familiar with this part of the district and the bus took a roundabout route before turning back towards where she lived. She was relieved, therefore, when she recognised landmarks and knew that the hospital wasn't far away.

When she alighted, the pavements were beginning to dry in the brilliant sun and little clouds of vapour were rising from them into the air.

"Quite a downpour, miss," the cheery porter said, when Alison reached the gate.

Alison managed a half-hearted smile. She was too worried about losing Tim to bother very much about the weather. She looked down at her legs, which were splashed with mud from the park. She could feel her long, brown hair clinging in wet strands about her neck. She didn't look half as smart as she looked the previous day. But, yesterday, she hadn't crawled through tunnels or run through the rain.

She decided not to mention Tim to her mother, for she hoped he would be safe with one of the neighbours by the time she returned home. If he wasn't, she didn't know quite what she would do. Should she call the police right away? Should she organise some of her school friends to comb the district until they found the runaway? Should she...

"Well!"

Suddenly, the decision she feared to make was taken from her. She stopped short in her tracks, put her hands on her hips and glared in front of her. Fifty yards away, half concealed by low bushes, a small figure crouched by the entrance to the block she wished to enter. It was a sorry-looking figure, damp, dirty, but very determined. She could see that from where she stood. The little boy clutched a roll of paper in his hands. Somehow, he had slipped passed the porter unnoticed. He was just about to make his entrance to see his mother.

"Timothy!"

Alison shouted at him and ran forward. She fell over her long umbrella. Picking herself up and rubbing a sore knee, she shouted again.

"Timothy! Wait!"

But he was nearer the entrance than she was. Like quicksilver, he slipped inside and, when she reached the door a few minutes later, he was nowhere to be seen.

CHAPTER SIX

TIMOTHY'S ESCAPADE

Alison paused in the entrance hall. She glanced up and down the corridors which led away into the heart of the block. They were empty. She felt worried and relieved; worried, because Tim's presence in the hospital was not allowed and she had to find him before anybody else did; relieved, because he was alive, safe and well. She felt angry and amused; angry, because of the unnecessary strain she had been put to; amused, because Tim had looked so comical. But this was not a time for feelings. Action was demanded. She had to be quick.

The ground floor was used as offices and she heard the tip-tap of a typewriter as she passed one room on her way to the staircase. She peered up the stairs which wound right to the top of the building. She hoped Tim would be peeping down at her, but he wasn't. She climbed to the next floor and looked down a similar corridor to the one she had left. There were more signs of life here. She decided to walk the whole length and climb the stairs at the other end. The building was constructed to a uniform design. There were little alcoves in one wall, just big enough for a boy to conceal himself, but Timothy wasn't there. She reached the far end unchallenged, until she met a nursing sister coming down from the next floor.

"And where are you going?" the sister asked. "Have you lost your way?"

Alison felt like a naughty schoolgirl who had just been caught red-handed by the headmistress.

"I have come to visit my mother in ward B3."

"Then you should have used the lift. The ward is two floors higher than this."

Alison mumbled her thanks.

"I shall be able to find it now," she said, as she continued up the stairs, conscious that the sister was still staring at her retreating figure.

"Phew!"

Alison reached the safety of the next floor and decided to use the lift. She felt very hot and bothered. Tim would have to be found later. She must see her mother without further delay.

When she found the lift, the indicator showed that it was coming up from the ground floor. It was slow-moving but she waited patiently. When it came she had a big surprise. A little face peered out at her through a small glass window as the lift glided smoothly by. Timothy waved to her as she stood watching helplessly.

"Timothy!"

She shook her umbrella at him and made signs for him to bring the lift down again, but, before she could make him understand, he disappeared from view. She watched the indicator. The lift went right to the top of the building. There was a brief pause, then, to her great relief, it began its downward journey. She pressed the call button and waited to give her brother a piece of her mind. But, when the automatic doors opened, she discovered that the lift was empty. Very angry, she stepped inside and rode up to the third floor.

"Hello, Alison."

A nurse greeted her as she stepped out into the corridor by the general ward. Alison smiled weakly. She nearly asked the friendly nurse if she had seen a dishevelled little boy, but she just stopped herself in time.

"The sister wants to see you again," the nurse continued.

Alison's face clouded.

"You won't have to wait for her today," the nurse added, guessing what was in Alison's mind. "Sister is in her office down the corridor."

"Thank you," Alison replied, finding her voice at last. "I'm very late today."

The nurse smiled.

"Never mind. I am sure sister will let you stay a little longer than yesterday. Your mother is greatly improved."

Alison was thrilled with these wonderful words. It was the first good news of her day. She knocked on the door of the office.

"Come in. Oh, hello, Alison. Do sit down a minute. You look tired."

The sister was very perceptive.

"I am tired," Alison admitted, readily. "I've had a dreadful day!"

"Were you caught in the storm?"

"Yes, I was."

Alison looked at a mirror which hung on the wall. She wanted to have a look at herself in it.

"Go on," the sister said. "I don't mind if you tidy your hair. Then I'll take you along to see your mother."

Alison smiled her thanks. She was beginning to like the sister very much.

"How is that young brother of yours?"

Alison adjusted her hair before replying. Then, suddenly, she decided to tell everything. When she had finished she felt much better.

The sister laughed heartily.

"Poor you! You have had a bad day! But I can assure you the young rascal isn't on my floor. Nobody passes this office without my permission. I think I'll telephone the attendants downstairs so that they can keep a look out for him. It wouldn't do to have a young boy wandering everywhere in the hospital, now, would it? He can't do much harm in the corridors."

"He won't get into trouble, will he?" Alison asked anxiously, wondering if she had done right in telling the sister about Tim's escapade. "He only did it to try to see Mother," she explained.

"Well, I shall give him a good telling off when I get hold of him," the sister said, with a twinkle in her eye. "But I think such an enterprising young man deserves some reward, don't you? I'll ask the porters to bring him up here and then he can see his mother."

"Oh, could he? That will make him very happy!"

The sister laughed again.

"I think it will make you happy, too. I can see that you are very fond of your brother."

She went off to telephone and came back shortly afterwards.

"That didn't take long," she said. "Come along now, Alison. We have kept your mother waiting too long. I'll bring Timothy in when he is found. You can stay for half an hour today."

They walked along the corridor, past the main ward and the anterooms, to the intensive care unit.

"We shall move your mother out of here, tomorrow," the sister explained, when they reached the small ward.

She opened the door and frowned. Alison stood in silence. Somebody was talking to her mother in a hushed, high voice. The sister stepped forward and gently pulled the screen curtain aside at one corner. Tim was sitting on a chair facing his mother. His soggy paintings were strewn across the floor and he was holding the best one in his hand. His mother was admiring it. The sister let the curtain go. She was amazed!

"However did he get in here?"

"And how did he know which room?" Alison added.

Suddenly, the sister put her handkerchief to her mouth.

"I should be cross," she whispered, trying to look stern. "But the sight of him sitting calmly with those paintings ... well! I'm lost for words!"

She pushed Alison forward.

"Go on," she said. "You had better join him. I'll come back when I have recovered."

"Hello, Mum."

Alison leaned across the bed to kiss her mother.

"Sorry I'm so late, Mum," she continued. "The sister wanted to have a few words with me."

She looked hard at Tim, hoping he would realise how cross she had been, but he seemed completely relaxed and undisturbed.

"I expect sister wanted to tell you what good progress I've made," her mother said. "I feel ever so much better today."

"You look fine!" Alison said, warmly. "God is answering our prayers."

"He knew we couldn't do without you," Timothy said, happily. "When are you coming home?"

Their mother laughed.

"God is good," she replied. "And, remember, even if He hadn't allowed me to get better. He is still good. He knows what is best for those who follow Him. Sometimes, we pray for what we want instead of asking that His plan for our lives, whatever it might be, will not be hindered."

Timothy looked thoughtful.

"I'm quite sure Alison is looking after you very well, Tim," their mother continued. "You must do all you can to help her."

Even Timothy blushed at that remark! And Alison maintained a loyal silence.

"The sister says I'll be able to come home in ten days or so. And Daddy will be home soon. He may be on his way now."

"I hope he arrives before Saturday," Timothy said.

"So do I."

Their mother turned to Alison.

"Tim told me you had thought of cancelling your holiday because of me," she continued. "You mustn't do that, Alison. You can see how much better I am, and, if Daddy doesn't arrive home in time, Tim can stay at his friend's house for a few days. I'll write a letter tomorrow when I feel stronger."

Alison didn't know what to say. She was annoyed with Timothy for trying to arrange everything. She had already made up her mind to stay in London while her mother was ill. Besides, she had written the fateful letter. Her holiday was off. But she couldn't bring herself to break the news to her mother, who, selfless as ever, was thinking of her daughter's happiness before her own.

"What did you think of Tim's pictures?" Alison asked, changing the subject.

"Very good! I like the one of the soldiers parading in front of Buckingham Palace. I can almost hear the music of the band. It looks so real."

Alison laughed.

"Show me, Tim. I haven't seen it yet."

Before long, the sister returned.

"I'm afraid it's time to go," she said. "But you may come back tomorrow, Alison."

"Thank you, sister," Alison replied. "Mum looks so much better today, doesn't she?"

"She is doing splendidly!"

Mrs Bennett smiled.

"It was so nice of you to bend the rules and to let Tim come," she said, innocently. "Seeing his paintings has done me the world of good."

The sister looked at him.

"Would you like to leave one of your paintings for your mother to look at?" she asked. "Choose the best one and I will stand it where your mother can see it."

Timothy chose the painting of the guards on parade.

"There you are, Mum," he said, proudly. "I knew you would like that one best of all, so I wrapped it inside the others to keep it dry. It rained so hard."

"Thank you. Tim. I shall enjoy having it in my room. Perhaps sister will let you come again when Daddy returns."

Alison looked at the sister's face. It was a picture of tact.

"Yes. Perhaps he can come in on Sunday," she said. "With his father, of course!"

"Dad won't be home by then," Timothy murmured, miserably.

They said goodbye and left the ward. Timothy suggested that they went straight home, but the sister had other plans.

"I want a few words with you first, young man," she said.

They went into the little office and the sister closed the door. Alison picked up her umbrella and twisted it around in her fingers. She felt awkward. She knew Timothy was in for a telling off.

"And, what I want to know is..."

"Well, how did you do it?" Alison asked, when they were standing outside the hospital, waiting for a bus. "You didn't tell the sister how you walked past her office without being seen."

Timothy was very subdued.

"If I tell you, you will tell her," he said, rudely.

"I might."

Alison wasn't making any promises.

"Well, I'll tell you," he said, at last, after the bus had arrived and they were seated on the top deck.

Alison smiled to herself. She knew he wouldn't be able to keep his secret for long.

"I didn't walk past," he said, proudly. "You know those big laundry baskets they use."

Alison looked horrified.

"You didn't hide in one of those!"

Timothy nodded.

"Yes," he boasted. "It was easy to slide past the porter while his back was turned. I ran into the lift as soon as I saw you, I knew you would be terribly angry."

"I was," Alison said.

"I went up and down in the lift several times and when I reached the top for the third time I jumped out. I saw two men coming down the corridor but they were busy talking to each other and they didn't see me. There was an empty laundry basket standing by the lift. I lifted the lid and jumped inside."

"Didn't they notice it was heavy?"

Timothy shook his head.

"No! There were two of them, and I don't weigh as much as you do!"

Alison poked him.

"They put the basket back in the lift, went down to the third floor, carried it right past sister's office and dumped it in the room next to Mum's. When they had gone, I climbed out of my hiding place, opened the door and peeped inside the next room."

"But you didn't know Mum was in there when you opened the door."

"No. Of course I didn't. Wasn't it lucky?"

Alison didn't reply. She didn't believe in luck. Perhaps Tim was meant to see Mum, after all. He had certainly cheered her with his paintings.

When they alighted, the sky was cloudy again and the shoppers in the main road were eyeing the black clouds cautiously. Everybody seemed to be scurrying around in an effort to finish their shopping before the next deluge. Alison, who had intended to do some shopping, decided to hurry home with

Tim and to go out again, later, when the sun came out. They had both received a severe soaking during the afternoon.

They reached home just in time. Alison opened the door as the first drops splattered on the garden path to send the spiders and other small creatures to the shelter of the nearest leaves. There was a letter on the mat.

"It's from Dad!"

Timothy picked it up.

"I expect it's to say he will be home tomorrow," he continued.

Alison stood her umbrella in the corner and took the letter. She opened it feverishly

"Be careful of the stamp," Timothy warned. "Don't tear it!"

The rain drove against the hall windows and, once again, lightning split the sky.

"Come into the dining-room, Tim."

It felt safer in the back of the house.

"Well, what does Dad say?"

Timothy couldn't restrain himself.

"Dad wrote this before he heard about Mum," Alison replied, sadly. "He was just supervising the loading of a truck and then he was going into the interior for a few days before flying home."

Timothy looked glum.

"So Dad won't be home tomorrow," he said. "There isn't a hope of him coming home before Saturday."

Alison shook her head.

"I doubt if he will be home before next Tuesday.

Never mind; I had decided to stay, and we can manage very well until Dad comes."

Alison was being very brave.

"But, your holiday!"

Timothy looked as if he were going to cry.

"You do want to go, really. I know you do!"

CHAPTER SEVEN

A WONDERFUL SURPRISE

After tea, the rain stopped. Alison went to the shops, armed with some money which her mother had instructed her to take from the bureau. Timothy didn't go with her. He wanted to watch a favourite television programme.

"I'll look after the house," he joked, settling down comfortably in the big armchair normally reserved for his father.

Alison couldn't help smiling. Despite the telling off he had received from the sister at the hospital, he was as bouncy as ever. Perhaps it had something to do with the fact that he had not been able to bring home his school report, which usually spoke of his enthusiasm but warned of his lack of concentration.

"All right, Tim," Alison said. "I may be quite a while, because the supermarket will be very crowded. They give double trading stamps today."

But Timothy hardly heard. His concentration, when watching television, lacked nothing. With a wave of his hand and a quick glance, he dismissed her, like a ruler dismissing a slave. Alison shrugged her shoulders and walked out of the house.

The air was sweet and fresh. Rain still dripped from the almond trees which stood at the edge of the pavement. The birds were singing their grateful thanks for all the worms that had come to the surface of the soil.

Alison hurried along and tried to remember all the things she had to buy. She wished she had stopped to make a list before leaving, especially when she entered the crowded supermarket. It was impossible to see all the things she wanted, at a glance, and it was difficult to reach the articles. Everybody seemed to be pushing everybody else.

"Hello, Alison," somebody called to her from the middle of a crowd of women at the bacon counter. When Alison looked up, she saw two girls from her class. She greeted them quickly and edged away. She didn't want to talk; to explain. She felt bitterly disappointed. Timothy had hit upon the truth. Of course she wanted to go to Kenya!

"Won't be long now, Alison," one of her friends called. "Have a good trip!"

Alison waved and pressed on. She didn't want them to know that she wasn't going. When she escaped from the shop, she strode home, lugging the heavy baskets until she was quite out of breath.

"Looks as if you have enough for a month there," one of the neighbours called.

"It is rather heavy. I should have taken Tim with me."

But Timothy was still intent on his programme.

"Have a look in the kitchen," he called, when he heard Alison in the hall.

She did as she was told. A large cake tin stood on the table. She opened it.

"Another cake!"

Timothy who had opened the serving hatch and was peering through, smiled broadly.

"Mrs Brown brought it," he said. "Doesn't it look super! It's got walnuts on top!"

Alison put the lid firmly back in place.

"We shall not cut it until the other one is finished," she said. "But, it's very nice of Mrs Brown. I must go and thank her."

"She said not to bother," Timothy said. "She is glad to be of help."

"All the same, I'll go."

When Alison returned, she found that Timothy had stirred himself into being helpful. He had put all the tinned food in the cupboard and stacked the items for the refrigerator in a neat pile.

"I've put the 'fridge things separate," he explained. "I thought it would be best if you put those away."

Alison beamed.

"Thank you, Tim," she said, warmly. "Perhaps we shall have a slice of that cake for supper, after all."

As the evening passed, Alison became more cheerful. After Timothy had gone to bed, she busied herself doing all the little jobs which needed to be done. For once, Timothy seemed ready for sleep, and the cooler weather, which had come with the rain, was a great help. She was able to work undisturbed, and she made excellent progress. When, very late, she crept up to bed, she fell asleep as soon as she had said her prayers. She planned to have a good rest in the morning, for Timothy wouldn't have to go to school.

She was in a deep sleep, therefore, when she heard somebody call. Slowly, she roused herself and listened. It was Timothy! She switched on her lamp and looked at the clock. Half past two! What a dreadful hour to be woken up! Sleepily, she slid out of bed and groped her way along to her brother's room. He had had another bad dream.

"What is the matter, Tim?"

He looked up tearfully.

"I've been dreaming again," he cried. "A horrible storm."

Alison stroked his forehead.

"A drink, perhaps?" she asked.

He nodded.

She walked to the bathroom for some water. She smiled to herself and then yawned. She knew how to deal with Tim now. She knew the routine.

"Here you are, Tim. Drink this and I'll shake your pillow."

He sat up, gulped down the cold water, and leaned forward so that she could make his bed more comfortable. She turned his pillows and, immediately, felt something stiff. It was a letter. Without letting him see, she hastily stuffed it in her dressing-gown.

"You must go straight back to sleep now," she said, firmly. "And please don't wake too early in the morning. I am so tired."

She went back to her room, closed the door and

took the letter from the folds of her gown. Her worst fears were confirmed, for, as soon as she had felt the letter in the half darkness, she thought it was her own.

"Oh, no!"

Timothy hadn't done what he had promised. He hadn't posted it! The organisers of the holiday wouldn't know that she was unable to go. Her first thought was to burst into Timothy's room and to face him with his deceitfulness. But she stopped herself in time. Wearily, she climbed back to bed, buried her face in her pillow, and quietly sobbed herself to sleep. She would have slept on and on, but for Timothy.

She heard his voice while she was still asleep. When she tried to open her eyes, before she was properly awake, she couldn't. She had a headache, too. But something about Timothy's voice made her stir. She managed to get one eye open when he burst into her room.

Alison looked at him blankly.

"What's wrong now? What's the time?" she yawned.

"It's nine o'clock in the morning! And, guess who's here?"

But Alison didn't have to guess. She looked beyond Timothy through the open door. A tall man with a bronzed face stood on the landing, smiling at her. She sat up in bed, stretched out her arms, and he came in. Quickly. She hung on to him, as though frightened that he would drift away like a dream.

But she knew he was real. And she still hung on. It was a long time before she spoke, and when, at last, she found her voice, she said just one word.

"Dad!"

Timothy watched happily.

"Now you really will be able to go!" he said, quietly.

When Alison recovered from her first unbelievable delight at seeing her father so unexpectedly, she insisted on preparing his breakfast while he talked to Timothy. She busied herself in the kitchen and hummed a catchy tune, an indication of the relief and overwhelming happiness in her heart. Everything seemed to be just right. The bacon cooked beautifully; the eggs didn't splatter all over the frying pan; the tomatoes didn't stick; the mushrooms were done to a turn. When her father looked in to see how things were going, he was met by a delicious aroma.

"It's nearly ready, Dad," Alison said.

"It smells marvellous! We have set the table. It'll be good to eat bacon and eggs again."

Alison laughed.

"You've only been away for three weeks," she chided.

They didn't hurry over breakfast.

"How did you manage to fly home so quickly?" Alison asked, when they were halfway through the meal.

"I thought you would want to know that. I was very fortunate indeed. I had planned to go into the interior to do a final survey with a colleague of mine.

We prepared all the equipment and packed all the sensitive instruments, and we were all set to go. The driver of the truck started the engine and we edged down the track, carefully avoiding the potholes so as not to damage the load. Then, when we were only three miles from field headquarters, the back axle went."

"And that was the end of your trip!"

Timothy knew that a back axle was a very important part of any vehicle.

"Yes, Tim. That was the end of our trip. There wasn't another truck suitable for the rough country we planned to explore, so we had to call off the survey."

"Does it make much difference to your report to the company?" Alison asked.

Their father shook his head.

"Not really," he said. "We just wanted to make quite sure of what we already felt was the best course of action. We have done all the aerial surveys, taken test bores and brought back all the mineral samples. It shouldn't be too difficult for the company chiefs to make up their minds."

"When did you first hear about Mum?"

"As soon as the cable reached Brazil! Do you know, I was actually in the company office when the message came through. In fact, I took the message myself. I drove to the airstrip in the little jeep in record time. I imagine the villagers thought I was mad. I begged a lift in a light plane owned by a Brazilian friend of mine, and we reached the main airport just in time. A jet stood on the runway, bound for Paris, and there was a vacant seat due to a last minute cancellation. If I had missed that plane, I shouldn't have been home until Monday."

They fell silent for a few moments.

"I think God meant me to catch that plane," their father continued. "But, now I am home, how is Mum? Tim has told me all about your visits."

Timothy didn't wait for Alison to reply, even though the question was addressed to her.

"Much better! And she has my best painting in her room."

Their father smiled.

"I am sure she's very pleased with it," he said. "I must hurry to the hospital now I have finished this excellent breakfast. I thought I must come home first, particularly as it is still quite early in the morning."

"They wake all the patients at half past six," Alison said. "And it's nearly ten o'clock now."

"Then I must be quick. I must have a wash and shave, then I'll take the car."

"You must look smart to see Mum," Timothy agreed. "Alison can go with you, then you won't waste any time finding the ward. It is is such a big hospital. Anybody could get lost in there, couldn't they, Alison?"

Timothy grinned broadly at his sister.

"I'll stay at home and do all the clearing up," he continued. "Alison really must go today. She must say goodbye to Mum before flying off to Africa!"

Alison started to protest, but her father interrupted.

"Good man, Tim! That is settled. Tomorrow, you and I shall have to manage on our own—that is, after we have seen Alison to the airport."

Alison went to her room to dress. She winced as she heard Timothy drop a plate, but she didn't care. She felt carefree. Her dad was home! Her trip was on! She took the letter Timothy had neglected to post and tore it into little pieces. She decided not to tell him what she had discovered under his pillow, although he didn't deserve to be let off.

While she waited for her father, Alison read a psalm.

"Praise the Lord, oh my soul: and all that is within me, praise His holy name!"

In a new and deep way, she could enter into the psalmist's own experience. Her heart was full of praise. The preceding days of anxiety seemed but a dream. She had been willing, if it was God's will, to miss her holiday, but He in His kindness had made it possible for her to go.

After their visit to the hospital and Alison had bid a fond goodbye to her mother, they drove home to collect Timothy. He had been true to his word and cleared everything away, beautifully.

"Come on, Tim! We are going out!"

There was no need to stay. Everything Alison

needed for her trip had been selected and packed early.

They drove eastwards out of London and joined the motorway to the Kent coast. The sky was clear and deep blue, flecked, here and there, by white, wispy clouds. The sun was high in the sky. The roof of the convertible was down. The wind pulled Alison's hair into untidy strands. Timothy sat tall in the back seat so as to feel the full benefit of the airstream as they sped along. Alison sat watching her father's big, brown hands gripping the wheel. Occasionally, he turned to smile at her, or to squeeze her hand. She felt liberated, as free as the swallows which whirled above them.

They reached the sea in time for a late lunch and they found a restaurant with big picture windows set high on the cliffs. It overlooked a sandy bay.

"No washing up to do!" Timothy said, when they had eaten. "Isn't it nice just to get up from the table and to walk away?"

Alison laughed.

"Now you know how much Mum does," she said.

They walked for miles along the clifftops. They walked until the waves below them became illuminated by the orange sun, which dipped into the sea to the westward. They walked until their lungs were full of the good, clean air. Then they recovered the car and drove back into the gathering darkness.

It was very late when they reached home, but they didn't mind.

"I expect you will both be too excited to sleep much," their father said.

But he was wrong. The air had done them good. Alison slipped into bed and listened to the movements her father made in the bedroom next to hers. She heard a click as he switched off the light, then a quiet thud as the bed knocked against her wall when he climbed in between the cool sheets. Deeply contented, she lay back and closed her eyes.

"Thank You for bringing Dad home," she said, quietly. "Thank You for helping me to trust You. Thank You, God, for everything. But please help Tim to remember what I told him that night when he had a bad dream. And please don't let him leave it much longer before he decides to follow You."

CHAPTER EIGHT

UP AND AWAY

Next morning dawned fine and clear. Long before they had to be, they were up and about. Alison was so excited, she could hardly eat her breakfast.

"I hope the weather stays like this for the flight," she said. "It would be nice to see the Alps from the plane."

"Perhaps you will be able to take a good photograph through one of the windows," Timothy suggested. "That would be super!"

The postman called after breakfast. There was only one letter. The envelope was foolscap size and buff in colour. Three words were printed on the reverse: "Greater London Council."

Timothy, who had rushed to the door, read them aloud.

"That is your report, Tim," Alison said.

Timothy pulled a face.

"I think we can leave that until later," he suggested.

They left to a chorus of good wishes from the friendly neighbours. The motorway west of London, though very busy, was wide enough to permit the heavy flow of traffic to speed along unhindered. Soon, they were aware of their nearness to the airport.

"That one was close!" Timothy shouted, as a huge plane whistled low overhead.

"Stick your fingertips in your ears!" Alison suggested.

They turned off the main road through the brightly lit tunnel, which went underground beneath the runways, and emerged right in the middle of the huge airport, close to the terminal buildings.

Timothy blinked in the strong sunlight.

"Look at all the people!" he gasped.

His father smiled.

"Aircraft arrive or leave every minute or two. It is just like a regular bus service," he explained.

They parked the car and carried Alison's luggage, inside, to be weighed and recorded.

"That is the last you will see of your cases until you arrive at Nairobi," the attendant remarked.

"Then, please put it on the right plane," Timothy said, looking anxious.

They all laughed, and went to book in and to wait in a passenger lounge.

Eventually, they were introduced to the other prizewinner and the television personality who was to accompany the two young people on their safari. Then it was time to say goodbye.

"Look after Mum," Alison said, as she kissed her father.

"You look after yourself!"

"And don't forget to take some good photographs," Timothy said. "And send us lots of cards and don't go too near the animals and—"

"I'll do everything you say, Tim," Alison said, as she bent down to kiss him.

After Alison had left the lounge, they went up to the rooftop to have a good view of the plane when it took off. They saw Alison step on to the tarmac and walk the short distance to the giant jet, which stood like a huge, metal fish, gleaming in the sun.

"She is waving!" Timothy said, jumping up and down.

They waved back, and Timothy's father lifted him high in the air so that Alison could see her brother clearly. They watched her walk up the gangway and step into the interior of the plane.

"I believe I can see Alison at one of the windows," Timothy said. "It's too far away to be certain, but I think it's her."

After a few minutes, the engines suddenly roared into life. Ever so slowly, the plane turned to taxi to the side runway. Five or six other planes were waiting permission to take off.

"The aircraft have to queue to leave!" Timothy exclaimed.

They watched the first planes go up, with great interest, but, when it came to the turn of the most important plane of all, they leaned forward in deep concentration. Timothy clutched his father's hand and, for once in his life, stood perfectly still.

Alison had already fastened her seat belt. The waiting period seemed endless. Would the aircraft ever fly? She sat looking out of the small window at the smooth concrete runway. Then, suddenly, she noticed the runway sliding by. As easily as a bird, the huge plane's nose tilted upwards and they were in the air.

"There she goes!"

Timothy and his father watched. Their hands shielded their eyes from the sun. They watched until the plane was a speck in the distance, like a fly. They watched until it disappeared into the heat haze.

"Wasn't that a smooth take-off!"

Timothy released his hot hand from his father's.

"Super!" he replied. "I knew you would be home in time, Dad!"

His father laughed.

"I think God knew Alison needed her holiday," he said.